My Name is Emma

A Collection of Stories about People who Share my Name

By Allison Dearstyne

Dedicated to every girl named Emma. May you be wholly known and wholly loved.

The name Emma has Germanic roots, coming from the word "ermen", which means universal or whole. Your name first became popular in England after the Norman conquest in 1066 when Emma of Normandy was the Queen of Denmark, Norway and England. Centuries later, in 1815, Jane Austen published a novel called *Emma,* where the main character, Emma Woodhouse, is a matchmaker. Your name has quite a history! There are wonderful women who have shared your name through the centuries, and we will look at these seven:

Emma Lazarus
Emma Gatewood
Queen Emma of Hawaii
Emma Didlake
Emma Azalia Smith Hackley
Emma Hwang
Emma Willard

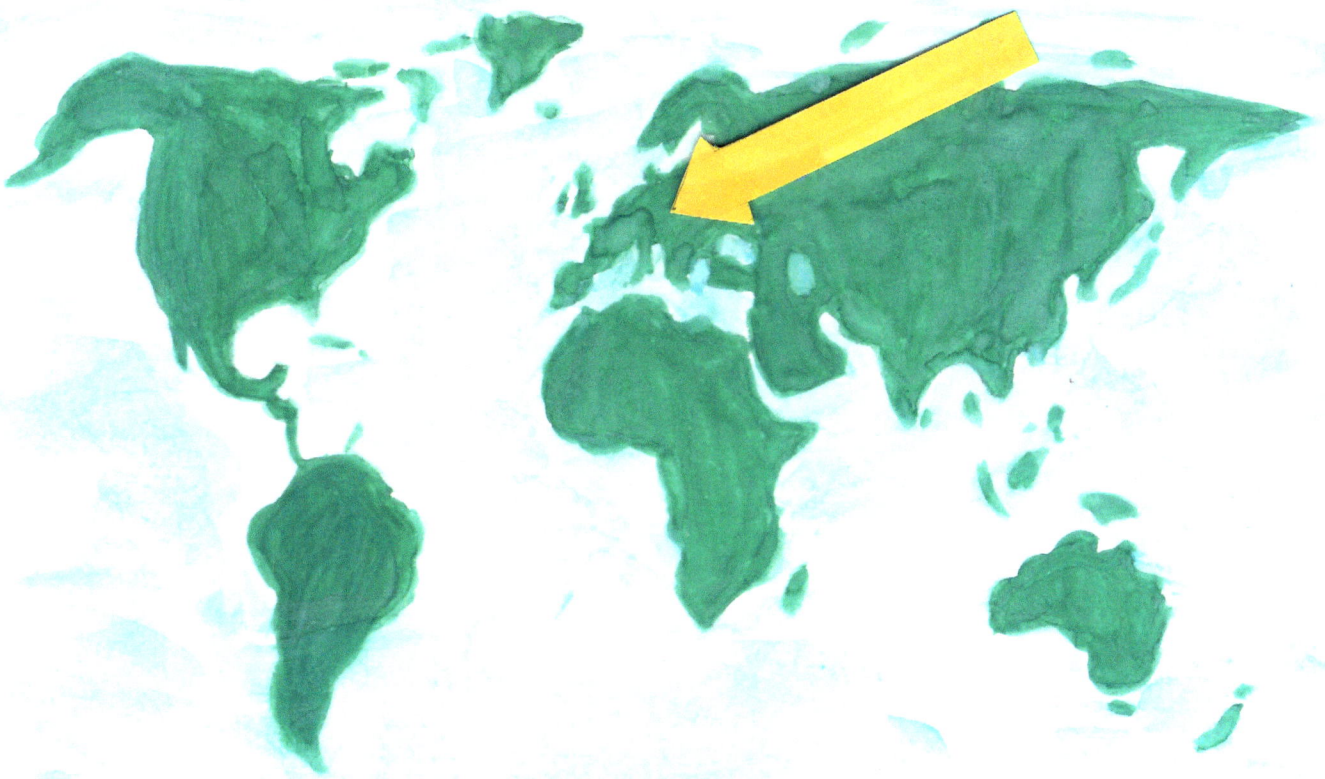

Emma Lazarus was the activist and poet who wrote the famous sonnet engraved on the Statue of Liberty. Born in New York City in 1849, she was the fourth of seven children to wealthy Jewish parents. From the time she was a little girl, Emma Lazarus loved to write. She wrote her first lyrics when she was only 11 years old! As a teenager, she wrote poems about the American Civil War, and was praised by many famous politicians and writers of her day. American author Ralph Waldo Emerson became a mentor to her.

As a young woman, her work became recognized overseas. She wrote on a variety of topics in many different formats - poems, articles, novels, and plays. A whiz in languages, Emma Lazarus spoke English, German, French, and Italian. There was one topic that began to fascinate her more and more in her career as a writer - her Jewish roots. She wrote about the mistreatment of the Jews through the millennia and their strong spirit, nevertheless.

Around the world racism against Jews was increasing. Specifically, Jews were driven out of Russia in 1881 and many immigrated to the United States. Emma Lazarus strove to help Jewish refugees and became an activist, which is someone who campaigns to bring about political and social change. She helped establish the Hebrew Technical Institute in New York, which provided training for Jewish refugees to support themselves.

Then in 1883, Emma Lazarus wrote her most famous sonnet *The New Colossus,* which was written to help raise funds for the Statue of Liberty's construction. She actually wasn't too keen on the idea until a friend told her that the statue would have great significance to immigrants sailing into the harbor. Wanting to inspire poor immigrants and welcome them to the United States, Emma Lazarus wrote:

"Give me your tired, your poor,
Your huddled masses yearning to breathe free.
Send these, the homeless, tempest-tost to me,
I lift my lamp beside the golden door!"

These famous lines have shaped American views on immigration and freedom to this day. It helped Americans to be sensitive to the needs of immigrants, who deserved to be treated with dignity and welcomed as friends. The Statue of Liberty was a gift to the United States from France. It was constructed by Gustave Eiffel, the architect of the Eiffel Tower. Lady Liberty is a Roman liberty goddess who holds a torch above her head and carries a tablet inscribed with the date of the United States Declaration of Independence. At her feet lies a broken chain. All of these are symbols of freedom in the United States. But it was Emma Lazarus who made the Statue of Liberty a welcoming symbol to immigrants arriving from overseas.

During the same year she wrote *The New Colossus,* Emma Lazarus founded the Society for the Improvement and Colonization of East European Jews. For the rest of her life, she dedicated her time to helping Jewish immigrants through education and advocated for them.

Emma Lazarus left behind quite a legacy! When you see the Statue of Liberty, think about the wonderful things it represents and think about Emma Lazarus!

Emma Gatewood was the first woman to hike the entire Appalachian Trail. She was born in 1887 in Ohio to a huge family with 14 brothers and sisters. Emma Gatewood married young and had 11 children, who she often took on walks through the woods. Emma Gatewood's life was hard, and walking through the woods calmed her. It gave her a sense of peace.

In 1950, Emma Gatewood read an article in *National Geographic* about the Appalachian Trail, the world's longest hiking trail through the world's oldest mountain range. The trail runs from Georgia to Maine and has shelters at the end of each day's walk. Emma Gatewood thought about hiking the trail for five years, and then at the age of 67, she told her adult children that she was going for a walk. Her children didn't ask for how long or where, because they knew that she was tough and could take care of herself. They didn't think she would walk 2,168 miles! The article in *National Geographic* gave her the impression of easy walks, and in retrospect, she said that they weren't easy!

Emma Gatewood didn't bring much with her on the trail. She wore Keds, which are simple canvas sneakers. She made herself a denim bag, which she carried slung over one shoulder. In her bag was an army blanket, a raincoat, and a plastic shower curtain, which as far as she was concerned, was all she needed. She didn't think she needed a tent, and sometimes spent nights under picnic tables, or on the ground. For a woman her age with her limited gear, Emma Gatewood kept a remarkable pace, hiking an average of 14 miles per day. She began hiking before sunrise and didn't stop until she was completely exhausted. Boy Scout troops and their leader who hiked a section of the trail reported that they could not keep up with Emma Gatewood!

"Granny Gatewood" became her trail name, and she began gaining some followers who loved her story. Local newspaper stories became national headlines, and she became a celebrity before her hike was over. Strangers became friends, giving her "trail magic," which is hiker lingo for food and places to stay. She finished the trail on Mount Katahdin after 146 days and was met by reporters who let her know how much of America was pulling for her.

Once she finished, national television shows interviewed her. She decided to hike the entire Appalachian Trail again when she was 72, and then again when she was 75. The Appalachian Trail Conference credited her for being the first female thru-hiker, and later for being the oldest female thru-hiker.

Emma Gatewood also hiked the 2,000-mile Oregon Trail, which runs from Missouri to Oregon. At 83, she was asked what she thought about the latest lightweight backpacking gear.

Emma Gatewood gave this advice: "Make a rain cape, an over the shoulder sling bag, and buy a sturdy pair of Keds tennis shoes. Stop at local groceries and pick up Vienna Sausages… most everything else to eat you can find beside the trail."

So, get outside and hike a few miles on a trail! Only carry the things you need for the hike, and you can be like adventurous Emma Gatewood!

Queen Emma of Hawaii was the cultured and compassionate wife of King Kamehameha IV of Hawaii. She was born in 1836 in Honolulu. Back in those days, Hawaii was its own country ruled by its own kings and queens. Royal from birth, her father was the High Chief, and her mother was the High Chiefess. As a little girl, she was often called Emalani, which means "royal Emma."

Emma was well educated as a little girl and became quite accomplished by the time she was 20. She loved to sing, dance, play piano, and ride horses. Emma was uniquely cross-cultural, growing up in a world where her native Hawaiian culture was heavily influenced by British and American culture. As an adult, she was baptized in the Anglican church, drank tea, and befriended Queen Victoria of England. But she also embraced her Hawaiian culture. She wrote poetry in her native language, fished, hiked, camped out and earned the trust of her Hawaiian subjects.

In 1856, she married Kamehameha IV and two years later, she had a son, Prince Albert Edward. As Queen, Emma took great interest in helping her subjects through charities. She persuaded her husband to establish a public hospital to help the Native Hawaiians who suffered from foreign-borne diseases. She visited the patients at the hospital often. Recognizing the need to better educate girls, she founded the St. Andrew Priory School for Girls.

Sadly, tragedy struck when Queen Emma's son died as a little boy from illness and then her husband died a year later. It was during this time that she became closer friends with Queen Victoria in England. They sympathized with each other, as both women had lost their husbands and sons.

Throughout her life, Queen Emma saw herself as the protector of her people. She wanted to stop Hawaiian dependence on American industry and give Native Hawaiians a stronger voice in government. After her husband's death, she still wanted to rule Hawaii, so she ran in an election but lost against King Kalakaua. Although the Hawaiian people favored Queen Emma, the Legislative Assembly elected King Kalakaua, who favored policies dependent on the United States.

Gradually, Hawaii lost its independence to the United States. But Queen Emma's work was not a lost cause. She helped her people in so many ways, and acts of kindness are never wasted. There are always people around us who need help. Show kindness to them and you can be like compassionate Queen Emma!

Emma Didlake was a Black American World War II veteran who lived to the ripe old age of 111. She was born in Alabama in 1904. When she was a teenager, her family moved to Kentucky, where she married a coal miner. Together they had five children.

She grew up under segregation laws. Segregation is separating people by race. You probably have seen pictures of segregation in the United States. Black people could not drink from the same water fountains as White people. The best seats in public places were always reserved for White people. It wasn't fair! One day Emma Didlake helped change that policy.

In 1941, life changed for Americans when Japan attacked Pearl Harbor, drawing the United States into World War II. Two years later, Emma Didlake enlisted in the Army to do her part to help win the war. She heroically served as a private and a driver. By doing so, she helped to integrate the United States Army. That means she helped to bring an end to segregation by working alongside White Americans. For her work, she earned a lot of medals and honors. The military was integrated after World War II, but the struggle for racial equality in the United States continued.

Emma Didlake and her family moved to Michigan, where she lived for the rest of her life. She joined her local NAACP chapter, which stands for the National Association for the Advancement of Colored People. The NAACP was, and still is, an organization with the goal of helping Black Americans achieve equal treatment. Emma Didlake even had the privilege of marching alongside Dr. Martin Luther King, Jr. in Washington, D.C. in 1963! She was inspired by his famous "I Have A Dream" speech.

Her work for her country and fellow Black Americans continued through her life, and as an old lady, she was often recognized for her great contributions. She had the honor of being the oldest living World War II veteran and said the secret to her longevity was a diet filled with fruits and vegetables! In 2015, she visited President Barack Obama in the Oval Office.

When she died, Barack Obama said, "Emma Didlake served her country with distinction and honor, a true trailblazer for generations of Americans who have sacrificed so much for their country." So, fight for what is right, eat your fruits and vegetables, and you can be like trailblazing Emma Didlake!

Emma Azalia Smith Hackley was a Black American singer and political activist. She was born in Tennessee in 1867 and loved music as a toddler. She became a child prodigy, which means she was extremely talented as a child. She played piano at the age of three and became a gifted singer and violinist as a little girl. Noticing her talent, many people suggested to her that she should claim to be White, to help her advance her career. After all, she did have light skin and hair. But she would not deny her Black heritage and remained proud of her roots despite what others said.

She moved with her parents to Michigan and graduated from high school. Then she became a schoolteacher and married Edwin Henry Hackley, a newspaper publisher and attorney from Colorado. Her husband's work inspired her, and they co-founded several organizations dedicated to helping Black Americans. She became the first Black American to graduate from the Denver School of Music in 1900.

Within a year, she devoted herself to a new mission in life - to educate Black Americans in classical culture. Believing this would help lift them out of poverty, she described herself as a "race musical missionary." She traveled throughout the United States and held concerts singing "negro spirituals," training local performers to sing with her. Emma Azalia Smith Hackley also gave local performers free classes on voice culture, and lessons on many other aspects of life. Through her classes, she emphasized the importance of being people of character.

She wrote books and articles on etiquette and her views that pride and self-help would lead to the racial uplift of Black Americans. Carry yourself with great dignity and be proud of your culture, just like Emma Azalia Smith Hackley!

Emma Hwang is an Asian-American scientist and aquanaut. She was born Yu-Liang in Taiwan in 1971. She moved to the United States when she was two and was called Emma. Growing up along the Texas Gulf Coast, she became interested in aerospace, which is technology concerned with space flight.

She earned a bachelor's degree, a master's degree, and a Ph.D. in biomedical engineering. That's a lot of years of hard work in school! While in college, she earned a second master's degree in electrical engineering, taught martial arts, and developed new medical techniques using ultrasound.

After graduating, Emma Hwang worked for Wyle Laboratories for the space industry. Astronauts often feel dizzy, nauseated and off-balance when they return to earth from space. She helped astronauts fix the problems of balance control that they experienced. She began scuba diving, and especially loved to dive in the Caribbean.

In 2003, Emma Hwang became an aquanaut, which is an undersea explorer who lives for a long time underwater. She lived in a laboratory sixty-two feet underwater for two weeks with some other aquanauts off Key Largo, Florida. Interestingly, the purpose of her work there was to prepare for future space exploration. Living in the deep ocean presents some of the same environmental challenges for crew members as outer space.

Emma Hwang is one amazing scientist! Pay close attention in your science class and you can be like smart Emma Hwang!

Emma Willard was a supporter of education for girls and the founder of a female academy that remains to this day. She was born in 1787 in Connecticut, the daughter of a farmer. She was inspired by her hard-working father, who encouraged her to read and think critically. She attended a local academy and became a teacher.

A few years into her teaching career, she moved to Vermont to head a female academy there. During her time in Vermont, she married a local doctor named John Willard and noticed that young women of her day were often denied a college education. Wanting to help these young women, Emma Willard opened the Middlebury Female Seminary in her home to provide them with an advanced education.

She wrote and delivered a speech, *Address…Proposing a Plan for Improving Female Education.* Some people made fun of her speech, thinking it was ridiculous that women should be taught scientific subjects, the same as men. But her speech played an important part in changing the mind of the public to become more progressive. More and more, people began to agree with her idea of advancing education of young women.

Her work continued when she moved to Troy, New York. Emma Willard opened the Troy Female Seminary, which was the first institution of serious learning for young women in the United States. After she died, the school was renamed the Emma Willard School, and it remains to this day!

Think about the many professions that women have these days, and how education makes that possible. We have pioneers like Emma Willard to thank for this!

This page is all about you!

_____ was born on

_____

As a baby, Emma _____

_____

As a little girl, Emma _____

_____

Emma is especially good at _____

_____

Emma is often described as _____

_____

Emma makes people laugh when she _____

_____

This page is for making a self-portrait. A self-portrait is a picture of you, drawn by you!

Bibliography

Biography.com Editors. "Emma Willard Biography." *The Biography.com website.* A&E Television Networks. 2 Apr. 2014. Web. 17 Oct. 2018.

Encyclopaedia Britannica Editors. "Emma Willard." *Encylcopaedia Britannica.* Encylcopaedia Britannica, inc. 8 Apr. 2018. Web. 17 Oct. 2018.

Jewish Women's Archive. "Emma Lazarus." *Women of Valor.* jwa.org. Web. 13 Oct. 2018

"Madame Emma Azalia Smith Hackley." *Historic Elmwood Cemetery & Foundation.* Where Detroit's History Endures. Web. 15 Oct. 2018

Peterson, Heather. "Hackley, Emma Azalia (1867-1922). *BlackPast.org.* Remembered and Reclaimed. Web. 15 Oct. 2018.

Seelye, Katharine. "Overlooked No More: Emma Gatewood, First Woman to Conquer the Appalachian Trail Alone." The New York Times. 23 Jul. 2018. Web. 6 Oct. 2018

Wikipedia contributors. "Emma (given name)." *Wikipedia, The Free Encyclopedia.* Wikipedia, The Free Encyclopedia, 12 Sep. 2018. Web. 6 Oct. 2018.

Wikipedia contributors. "Emma Didlake." *Wikipedia, The Free Encyclopedia.* Wikipedia, The Free Encyclopedia, 22 Sep. 2018. Web. 13 Oct. 2018.

Wikipedia contributors. "Emma Azalia Hackley." *Wikipedia, The Free Encyclopedia*. Wikipedia, The Free Encyclopedia, 18 Jan. 2018. Web. 15 Oct. 2018.

Wikipedia contributors. "Emma Hwang." *Wikipedia, The Free Encyclopedia*. Wikipedia, The Free Encyclopedia, 2 Oct. 2018. Web. 19 Oct. 2018.

Wikipedia contributors. "Emma Lazarus." *Wikipedia, The Free Encyclopedia*. Wikipedia, The Free Encyclopedia, 19 Sep. 2018. Web. 13 Oct. 2018.

Wikipedia contributors. "Grandma Gatewood." *Wikipedia, The Free Encyclopedia*. Wikipedia, The Free Encyclopedia, 17 Sep. 2018. Web. 6 Oct. 2018.

Wikipedia contributors. "NEEMO." *Wikipedia, The Free Encyclopedia*. Wikipedia, The Free Encyclopedia, 11 Oct. 2018. Web. 20 Oct. 2018.

Wikipedia contributors. "Queen Emma of Hawaii." *Wikipedia, The Free Encyclopedia*. Wikipedia, The Free Encyclopedia, 13 Jul. 2018. Web. 19 Oct. 2018.

Wikipedia contributors. "The New Colossus." *Wikipedia, The Free Encyclopedia*. Wikipedia, The Free Encyclopedia, 11 Sep. 2018. Web. 13 Oct. 2018.

www.ingramcontent.com/pod-product-compliance
Lightning Source LLC
Chambersburg PA
CBHW042111040426
42448CB00002B/221